Elliot

Mireia

Joey

Maisie

Isla

pda panda

THE **PANDA** ON **PDA**

The fantastic drawings of Pandas that we proudly display on the inner covers of this book have all been drawn by amazing children. Most of them are real Pandas themselves — autistic children with PDA (Pathological Demand Avoidance) — and the rest were done by their wonderful siblings and friends and advocates of Pandas. Rebecca and I are so thankful to all of you for making our book extra special. Thanks so much!

THIS BOOK BELONGS TO

by the same author

The Amazing Autistic Brain Cards
150 Cards with Strengths and Challenges for Positive Autism Discussions
Glòria Durà-Vilà
Illustrated by Rebecca Tatternorth
ISBN 978 1 78775 430 0

Me and My PDA
A Guide to Pathological Demand Avoidance for Young People
Glòria Durà-Vilà and Tamar Levi
Illustrated by Tamar Levi
ISBN 978 1 78592 465 1
eISBN 978 1 78450 849 4

My Autism Book
A Child's Guide to Their Autism Spectrum Diagnosis
Glòria Durà-Vilà and Tamar Levi
ISBN 978 1 84905 438 6
eISBN 978 0 85700 868 8

THE
PANDA
on PDA

A Children's Introduction to Pathological Demand Avoidance

Glòria Durà-Vilà

Illustrated by Rebecca Tatternorth

Jessica Kingsley Publishers
London and Philadelphia

First published in Great Britain in 2022 by Jessica Kingsley Publishers
An imprint of Hodder & Stoughton Ltd
An Hachette Company

1

A CIP catalogue record for this title is available from the British
Library and the Library of Congress

ISBN 978 1 83997 006 1
eISBN 978 1 83997 007 8

Printed and bound in China by Leo Paper Products

Jessica Kingsley Publishers' policy is to use papers that are natural,
renewable and recyclable products and made from wood grown
in sustainable forests. The logging and manufacturing processes
are expected to conform to the environmental regulations
of the country of origin.

Jessica Kingsley Publishers
Carmelite House
50 Victoria Embankment
London EC4Y 0DZ

www.jkp.com

To David and our children, Josep and Mireia, great advocates of Pandas.

Also, in memory of my father (1948–2021), who loved the early stages of this book

– Glòria

To James and our wonderful children, Roo and Finn

– Rebecca

Bears are the autistic family of the Animal Kingdom. We have many wonderful qualities. For example, we enjoy being alone at times, can be very independent, are fiercely loyal to our families and are peaceful until thoroughly annoyed. Oh, yes, and we also get lots of pleasure from our senses! Have you seen us rubbing our backs, shoulders and the back of our heads on trees or even telephone poles? (It feels so good!)

As there is great
diversity among autistic
people, this is also the
case among us bears. Look
at some of my friends – polar
bears, brown bears, black bears…
We have many things in common
but we can also be different and,
as I will show you in this book,

**we Pandas are a particularly amazing bunch
of bears!** Each bear is special but we Pandas have
a **particular style of autism** called **PDA** that
makes us extra-special. PDA is the name of the
Pandas' unique place on the autism spectrum.

It makes us so proud when the wonderful children, like **you**, who share our style of autism call themselves after us: the **Pandas**. You belong to such a terrific **tribe**!

Would you like to take the place of honour in this book and draw or stick a picture of yourself here?

....

Dr Glòria

Rebecca

We Pandas believe that **learning about ourselves** is VERY important as it will help us understand ourselves better and lead a happy life. I've asked **Dr Glòria**, a doctor of autistic children who is particularly fond of Pandas, to help me write this book (it was tricky for me to do the typing with my paws). As I wanted this book to be very beautiful for you, I have asked an artist called **Rebecca** to illustrate it; she really got me right. I thought you may like to know my **co-author** and **illustrator**. Here they are!

I Am Creative + Original

I Am Observant, curious + good with detail

I Am Honest, fair + just

I Am Caring + thoughtful

Let's start with a big fact: although Pandas have **lots** of things in common, we are all different. **No two Pandas are the same!** Shall we have a look at what makes us such a **cool autistic tribe**? I wonder which bits apply to you and which ones don't?

Before we concentrate on us, let's have a look at some of the things we have in common with other bears, as we are all family and we are all autistic. Bears, like all animals, have **strengths** (things we are awesome at) and **difficulties** (things we struggle with). Dr Glòria created these cards to show us **our very own** set of strengths (yellow cards) and challenges (blue cards). Here are mine. There are three blank yellow cards in case you want to add some of the things you are good at.

I STRUGGLE WITH making friends + getting along with others

I STRUGGLE WITH Understanding how I and others feel

I STRUGGLE WITH Certain noises, smells, fabric, food + lights

I STRUGGLE WITH Changes + Uncertainty

Did you know that Pandas were believed to have **special powers** in ancient China? We are indeed a unique gang of bears. If you feel like it, how about sharing with us the things you are **good** at? Maybe you or someone you trust could write them on these cards which we have left empty for you. Some of us may need our loved ones to remind us of our talents. I am sure they will be delighted to help you.

I AM

I AM

I AM

As you have just seen, you and I and our fellow Pandas have lots of talents and things we are good at (our yellow cards). I want now to share with you the things we Pandas **struggle** with a lot, as these are the things that make us worried and often get us into trouble. Many Pandas have shown this book to the grown-ups caring for them so **they can understand us better and give us the help we need**.

Let's start with our top challenge. Like every Panda, I find it **VERY VERY VERY hard** to do **what others tell me to do**. In fact, I hate it so much that I run away pretty fast and have become brilliant at climbing trees to escape people's demands!

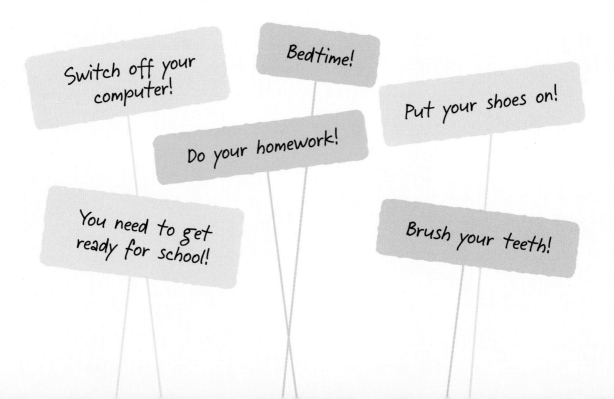

When I feel safe, I am peaceful, charming and fun, **but** if those around me keep pushing me to do things I cannot do and I cannot find a tree nearby to climb up, I can become **very angry** and look very fierce, as we Pandas have powerful jaws and teeth. Another feeling I often have is **anxiety**. When I am **anxious**, I feel worried and afraid. Some of us even feel it in our hearts, minds and bodies.

GRRRRRRRRRRRR!

Being asked to do things sometimes makes me feel **so terribly anxious** that I feel as if my life is just an endless list of demands. I hate feeling this way! When I feel this way, I just want to be **by myself**, become **very quiet**, not talk to anyone, go into a little ball and hide in a cave that will shut out all these demands.

I sometimes escape from it all by going into my own **fantasy or imaginary world** where I feel safe.

When someone asks me to do something that I know I am perfectly able to do, I sometimes feel as if I have two little 'mini-mes' inside my head, arguing with each other. One is telling me that I **CAN** do it and the other is shouting at me that I absolutely **CAN'T**.

I have noticed that when I am very stressed, the 'mini-me' trying to convince me that I **CAN'T** do something becomes **very loud** but when I am feeling calm it becomes **less** loud so I can start listening to the mini-me saying **'YES, YOU CAN DO IT!'**

YES, YOU CAN DO IT!

We Pandas need to **feel in control** to feel good. Rather than being told what to do, we love to be allowed to **do our own thing**. Unlike some bears, we Pandas don't hibernate as we want to have as much time as possible to do the things we love.

Pandas also often feel that they are **not given enough time to give an answer**. Many times, I have felt rushed to move on to something else before I could come up with a reply. I find it very annoying when people move on to another thing before I am ready to do so.

We are so great at doing our own thing that we have even developed special paws to hold our favourite food, bamboo shoots. We love it so much that we would spend 14 hours a day eating bamboo if we could! I also like spending time with my pet and playing with my trains and Lego. Doing the things I love not only makes me **happy** but it also makes me **cope better with the things I don't like doing**. I wonder which things you love doing? How about writing them on these bamboos, so all the grown-ups around you can **make sure you have enough time to do them**.

Being told what to do makes me feel so incredibly anxious and out of control that I have noticed that **without thinking** I do lots of things to protect myself from demands, like saying **'NO!'** immediately or **ignoring** them. I will share with you some of the things I have noticed I say to escape demands. I wonder if you also use some of them?

I can't have a bath now!

I need to finish my book

I don't have the right soap

I have become very good at **convincing** those asking me to do something **why** I can't do it. I often spend **lots** of time and energy giving excellent reasons for not doing what the grown-ups want me to do.

I will catch a cold

The towel feels rough

I am too tired

I will have a bath another day

At times, it is extremely hard for me to do what my parents and teachers ask me to do, even things I know I **CAN** do. This is so annoying! What is even **more** infuriating is not being able to get myself to do the things I really **WANT** to do!

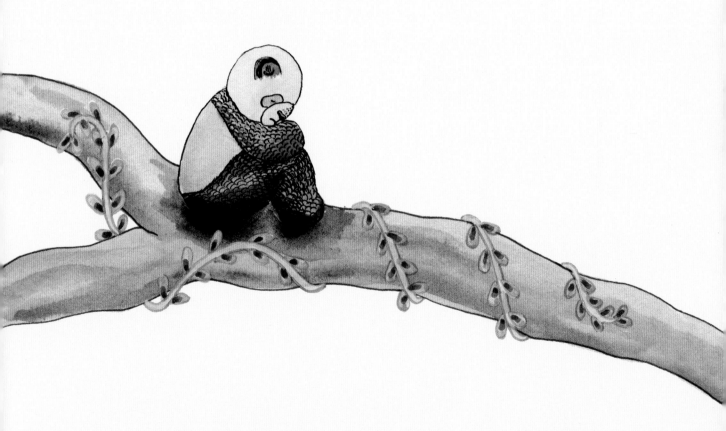

We Pandas like being by ourselves, doing our own thing, but we also like to be with others when **we** feel like it. We are very good at **leading** games and it is great fun when others play our games in the way we want. Some of us have a **special friend** that we like best. I have one, but I don't like it when my special friend plays with someone else at break time as I want my friend all for myself and I worry they may stop caring about me.

Some Pandas have very **active imaginations**. Some of us become part of the fantasy world of our favourite book, toy or film; we may have friends that others can't see; we may like to act as if we were someone else. Sometimes our imaginary life is more exciting, and also safer, than our real life and we spend lots of time there. I have sometimes been carried away by my imagination and it all got a bit confusing.

Some of us Pandas also use our **vivid imagination** to get out of demands, using role play or fantasy. For example, a Panda friend of mine who loves being a dog told their mum that they couldn't brush their teeth as dogs don't do such things. I once told my dad that I couldn't go to school as my favourite soft toy was poorly and I had to look after it.

When we are overwhelmed
by demands, we feel
so bad that we will do
anything to get out of
the situation. I have told
my parents that I couldn't
get out of the house as my
legs didn't work. I have also
shouted and said horrible
things to them. I have even
lost control of my actions
– as if a volcano inside me
exploded – and lashed
out. One time, I broke my
brother's favourite toy.

We Pandas have also noticed that having **too many things going on** around us makes doing the things we have to do more difficult.

If there are too many things happening around me, or too many people, I feel **more anxious** and I find it much harder to behave myself. I feel like this in supermarkets, and once I had a huge meltdown there. Grown-ups around us should take note of the places that make us feel this way so we can avoid them or we get the help we need to be okay there.

In my opinion, **I don't see why I should do what grown-ups tell me to do**. It doesn't make sense that I get into trouble when I don't do what adults ask me to do. **I am the boss of me!**

We Pandas like to be **in charge** and we love it when our parents, siblings and friends are our helpers and do the tasks we set for them. This makes us **feel in control**.

You have to follow the rules of my game!

You are my assistant!

I am the boss!

On a **good day**, when we are feeling calm, safe and in control, we Pandas can do the things that we struggle with on a **bad day**. When I am having one of those bad days and I feel stressed out and anxious, I even struggle with doing very small things.

I can't put my pyjamas on!

It is so important to learn which things make us Pandas have **bad days**. Good days are so much more fun! Let me share with you some things that I and my fellow Pandas have noticed can **turn a good day into a bad one** so those caring for us can help us to have lots of good days:

- Feeling anxious
- Feeling out of control
- Not being given choices
- Feeling tired
- Being put on the spot

- Struggling to cope with:
  - too much noise
  - annoying lights
  - bad smells
  - itchy clothes

Struggling to go to school is very common for us Pandas; it is full of things we have to do, everyone expects us to behave in a certain way and we are not allowed to do our own thing! No wonder we find it tricky to get ready on time, and we get into trouble when things get too much for us. Sunday evenings are hard as I worry about the week ahead and lie awake in bed, thinking of all the demands I will be facing the following day. Some of us find going to school so super hard that we just stop going.

Some Pandas want to **fit in** so much at school that they **force** themselves to do all the things they are asked to do. They are like **actors** playing a character, at school, in other places, or with certain people. It is like putting on a **mask**, not being who they truly are. When I do this, my anxiety becomes very high, I feel totally exhausted, and I end up exploding at home when I finally feel safe. We Pandas use our white fur to **camouflage**, to fit in, around snow, and our black fur around rocky places. Wouldn't it be so much better to be who we really are and be proud of the whole of our fur?! Grown-ups around us have the important mission to make places safe for us to **be ourselves**.

Children with PDA, just like us Pandas, **will thrive and lead happy, fun lives** in the right environment, when those around us help us in a way that fits with our unique style of autism. Panda experts know that when we are well looked after, we thrive. Dr Glòria is certain of this. Pandas need very personalized attention. Not all bears have the same needs and find the same things useful. In fact, things that are great for us Pandas are not so great for other bears! Now, after looking at all the things we struggle with, let's look at the ways the grown-ups around us could really help us with our challenges.

Here are some ways for the grown-ups to help us that I have found useful. I call them: **MY STRATEGIES**. I wonder which of them work for you? Dr Glòria has added some others that Pandas have taught her. Sometimes, grown-ups try to help us but don't get it right, but they can learn from you, the best teacher there is, what is helpful and what isn't. How about using this book to teach them how to help you?

- Give me choices; be flexible
- Don't make demands when I am anxious
- Don't rush me; talk in a clear way that I understand
- Create 'safe spaces' for me to go to when things get too much
- Make learning exciting; use my imagination
- Let me have a say in plans

This book is coming to an end but before I go back to my bamboo, I would like to share a very **cool fact** about Pandas. I often remind myself and the adults around me about this: although Panda cubs go through many struggles, needing lots of care and protection from other animals – so we don't end up in their bellies – when we are grown up and we have learned how to look after ourselves, we become mighty, magnificent Pandas **without** any natural predators! There are **no** animals who dare to eat us!

It is so important that those caring for us understand our struggles and give us the right help, especially when we are little, so we learn how to cope with our difficulties and develop our wonderful talents.

Now it is time for Dr Glòria and me to say **goodbye**. It has been a great pleasure to meet **you**. We firmly believe that learning about yourself and getting your strategies right will make you, wonderful Panda, into a…

SUPER PANDA!

Alex

Arijana

Poppy

Josep

Amelie